72 LESSONS

TO

ROCK YOUR LIFE

Encouragement for your life
and spirit

Copyright 2015 Sasha Woertz Westray

Copyright © 2015 Sasha Woertz Westray

All rights reserved. This book or any portion thereof may not be reproduced or used in any manner whatsoever without the express written permission of the author and publisher
except for the use of brief quotations in a book review.

Printed in the United States of America

First Printing, 2015

ISBN-13: 978-1515061229

ISBN-10: 1515061221

CreateSpace Independent Publishing

Cover Illustration Copyright © 2015 by Sasha Woertz Westray
Cover design by Sasha Woertz Westray
Author photograph by Sasha Woertz Westray

Disclaimers

Although the author and publisher have made every effort to ensure that the information in this book was correct at press time, the author and publisher do not assume and hereby disclaim any liability to any party for any loss, damage, or disruption caused by errors or omissions, whether such errors or omissions result from negligence, accident, or any other cause.

This book is not intended as a substitute for the medical advice of physicians. The reader should regularly consult a physician in matters relating to his/her health and particularly with respect to any symptoms/concerns that may require diagnosis or medical attention. The author and publisher take no responsibility for any issues that arise from the information within this book. It cannot ensure such exclusion and no liability is accepted. The reader is recommended to take all appropriate precautions before following any nutrition guidelines, fitness, or any information from this book. It is always recommended to check with your doctor first before starting any nutritional and/or physical fitness program. The author is not permitted to diagnose, or claim to treat, medical or mental conditions. Nutritional/fitness/life advice is not a substitute for professional medical advice and / or treatment. The reader is responsible for contacting their GP about any health, or mental concerns.

The information in this book is meant to supplement, not replace, proper fitness training. Like any sport involving speed, equipment, balance and environmental factors, any activity or fitness pose some inherent risk. The authors and publisher advise readers to take full responsibility for their safety and know their limits. Before practicing or applying any skills described in this book, be sure that you check with a doctor or receive medical advice, and do not take risks beyond your level of experience, aptitude, training, and comfort level. Any type of advice is not a substitute for professional medical advice and / or treatment.

Have you ever asked yourself, "Is this normal? Any reassurance and wisdom you can throw my way, please?"

I used to say that to all my friends and family when I was in my 20's. "There's not a guide on how to get from A to B to C!" You always hear the start and end result of all these awesome stories. You hear fabulous stories of careers, life goals, love and relationships, relocating, magical self- worth and confidence, settling down and calling a place home, and finding your purpose and calling. But, hello CAN SOMEONE TELL ME THE STEPS ALONG THE WAY!?! Does anyone have a blueprint I can see?

I wanted to connect, resonate, read, and feel that I was normal in all the feelings, experiences, and challenges I was facing. Reassurance and support, that this was part of the journey and can't be passed, but that the steps were glorious stepping stones.

We all want soul comfort and a sense of peace, while we are in seasons of our journey. We crave acknowledgement that we are supposed to be learning and growing and receiving tools that will blossom us! We want proof that we will benefit and be blessed through the journey.

We yearn for validation, affirmation, and acknowledgement that our trials are normal and we are OK.

The gift in this lifetime is to be our REAL DEAL authentic and awesome self. The gift is to hear our inner voice and know that our inner compass is developing and strengthening through the journey. We can truly believe all will be fabulous, and that these experiences are part of the process to benefit us. It will be more than just, "ok." It will be meaningful and for our good!

My feelings, thoughts, choices, and decisions with career, life, relocations, friends, love, purpose, passion, and all the in between of discovering who I WAS, what MY PURPOSE was, and what JOY meant to ME was sometimes full of rough seasons and experiences.

I have a BOAT LOAD of tools in my toolbox for life. I apply and use and LOVE them. I have shared and encouraged them with others.

Do you want to feel empowered, passionate, purposeful, inspired, wise, and joyful? Connect to your true self and your inner compass and allow the growing, learning, and applying of these life lessons to empower you. Use the tools. Life allows us to continue to receive new ones. The following lessons come from a place of love and encouragement. They can be used the rest of your life.

ONE THING ALWAYS REMAINS CONSTANT: Allow yourself to tune into your inner voice and LISTEN and FEEL that inner compass. Instinct. Soul. Spirit. Higher Power. Inner Voice. God. Jesus. Holy Spirit. WHATEVER YOU CALL IT. PLUG INTO AND USE IT. It guides you, it unconditionally has your back, and it reveals your true purpose and worth. Life is blessed and flows more easily from this place. Unlimited love is there and that is the realest it gets!

INSTINCT. SOUL. SPIRIT. HIGHER POWER. INNER VOICE. GOD. JESUS. HOLY SPIRIT. THE DIVINE. WHATEVER YOU CALL IT. PLUG INTO IT AND USE IT.

1. Knowing VS Thinking

Knowing something and thinking something are two different things. When you say, "I *know* I am guided. I *know* I am supported. I *know* I am loved. I *know* I am enough." It is a truth. It is activated. It is planted in power. When you *think* you are or aren't something, that can change according to your feelings or circumstances at the time. Truth is truth.

If you sabotage yourself by doubting, justifying, or wondering, then stop and observe you are doing this.

Speak truth. *I KNOW.* That has a power to it. That has a truth to it. Start using that in the way you talk to yourself, talk about your dreams, and speak in your life. Knowing the truth and living it has a different vibe to it, than experiencing, thinking, and wondering about it.

Tool: Speak or write I know I am... (guided, important, protected, safe, loved, enough)

2. Plant Seeds

I am a big believer and doer of planting seeds. Especially if you have over the top, huge, out of this world financial, emotional, physical, and powerful goals that seems enormous. No matter how small the seed is you plant, do it every day because they add up. The smallest little action daily adds up to BIG progress. Plus, allowing the Divine time and hand of God to water those seeds, and to allow space and outside forces to contribute; they blossom!
Regardless if the result is in the form that you want or in the time frame you want, they blossom!

Sometimes we all just need a soul tune up---reminder---that we are limitless, worthy, powerful, and life is to be amazing the minute you wake up!

I'm serious! It's not about having moments of joy or bringing joy INTO parts of your life. It's LIVING it always.

It's easy for all of us to get caught up in our everyday life and feel limited or question if we can have an amazing life like that. You can. Planting seeds daily that contribute to yourself, your visions, and your dreams are huge steps.

There is a vibrant, possible, thriving, and exciting world going on and you CAN have all the dreams and goals you desire. There isn't a magic blueprint. There isn't a follow these 5 steps and everything is fixed. Your vision has to go through steps and actions. Planting seeds every day no matter how small they seem, add up over weeks, days, months, and time. The next thing you know it is HAPPENING! Never underestimate the power of planting seeds in ALL areas of your life.

Tool: Do something right now that is in alignment with your vision. Write down an affirmation, say something out loud that is uplifting, make one phone call, take a breath and clear any thoughts that limit you, write one sentence for your new blog, do 10 sit ups (if you have weight loss goals), RIGHT NOW. Plant a seed NOW! They all count and all matter. Everything is significant and adds momentum to your goals.

Some of my affirmations to say is, "Is this serving my highest good?" "Is this true for ME?" "Does this align with MY beliefs and values and guiding light?" "Is this expanding and energizing my soul?"

3. In Just One Day

"We are born in one day. We die in one day. We can change in one day. And we can fall in love in one day. Anything can happen in just one day."
Gayle Forman

Life happens to all of us. Life doesn't discriminate against who you are. Disappointments, challenges, and sorrow, everyone experiences.

Life is short. Your days on earth are numbered.
Tomorrow is not promised. Life and its challenges will be happening all the time, no matter what age you are.
Don't save your nice perfume for just going out on the town.
Don't say when I lose 20 lbs. I'll wear my awesome outfit that I'm saving. Don't say, once I have the degree, I'll apply for that job I really want. Don't say, once I get A, I'll do B.
Do it all NOW NOW NOW! Today. Today. Today.
I mean it. What do you bring to the table?
"I bring the table to the table!" Say and believe that about yourself!

There's no perfection. No perfect conditions, nothing.
There is no one size fits all. And, you know what?
When we all were born, we were born; carefree, wild, beautiful, smart, and spirited.
We didn't want success. We didn't want the ideals of beauty. We didn't have a 5 step plan that made us feel important, smart, or worthy. We didn't want half of the things that everybody is wanting these days.
We were taught "that stuff". When we were born and a little kid, we just rocked our spirited SOULS. We rocked our voice and our creativity and what we liked and what we didn't like. We just marched to the beat of our own drum, our way.
We wanted love and our parents/caregivers to give us 100% total engaged attention and presence and love. Period.

We get taught to want certain things, do and perform at certain things, and to be a certain way with certain things.

Always remember that you being born is the best gift.
You still have all that amazing, carefree, peaceful, spirited love. Your beauty and power is inside of you to shine.

There isn't a one size fits all or one way of anything.
What do you want in your world right now? Is it aligned with what you have been taught or with what truly sings deep inside you? Is it truly your belief and value, or is it a conditioned pattern that no longer serves your highest good?

Know thyself! God created you in holiness.
Don't lose that in your experiences. We start to attach our worth with our experiences. If you make a mistake or fail at something or stumble and fall which is all part of being normal, we believe we suck, aren't smart, aren't enough, or not amazing. NOT TRUE! *Don't mistake your worth by your experiences!* Your true identity is holy, spirited, gorgeous, talented, and brilliant. You were made by Divine power and a Divine creative artist! Your soul is that FOREVER! Live life TODAY! Totally powerful and gorgeous YOU!

4. What is Your Language?

Do you resonate and understand things more through visual, verbal, written, art, movement, music, or expression? Find out. That is your language. That is what speaks most to your core. When this is identified, you can create much more action and momentum in your life, in your favor. Yes! Whether it is in school, work, your home, or however you receive information, knowledge, wisdom, or anything that moves your soul, find your language. You will know because it just comes easy and effortless to you, to retain the information in that form. Some people can recite word for word song lyrics because with the music flowing with it, it speaks to their heart. Some people love art and pictures and it stores in their mind like that. Some people do well, reading books or the written word and it resonates for them. Some take in wisdom through movement, touch, and the emotions it creates in their spirit, like through dance, sports, fitness, or creating art or doing a physical project and your body just take it in and "gets it".

Find your genius. Discover your language. A fish can't climb a tree, but it is an excellent swimmer. Once you deeply know your language, you can do and apply more of it to reach goals, dreams, inspirations, and create any change you want in your life.

Example: You are visual. You want a new home. Cut out pictures and post everywhere of houses that you like. Put up images of words that empower you towards that goal, like trust, faith, divine timing, home is where the heart is, etc.

See this visually daily and it will motivate you towards achieving it.

Tool: Identify your language. Take action on that language and do more of it. Show up in it and affirm it. This creates more action.

5. Life is Short. Rock Yours Now.

Life really is short. You have no idea when your days will be numbered. Why wait until you lose 20 lbs. to wear that outfit you are saving? Why wait until you have a special occasion to use your good perfume? Don't hold yourself back from a FULL and VIBRANT LIFE TODAY. Today is the day to truly embrace life! Wake up and seize the day, be excited to spread your vibe, your love, your gifts and talents. Rock your look, and do things that you always want to save for another day. There are no right conditions. THERE IS RIGHT NOW, because tomorrow is not promised. Yesterday is done. TODAY! Whatever truly lights you up and ignites your joy, do more of it, today. Don't waste time doing things that other people tell you is fun and important. What is important and fun to you? Life can pass by while you waste time doing what you think is expected of you, what you were taught is of value, and what doesn't resonate with your inner beliefs. That is a waste to live out someone else's definition of success, love, or a great life! DO YOU. Today rock your power, rock your unique and beautiful self, and LIVE!

6. Be Willing

Be willing to receive more of what life has to offer you and be willing to say yes. Be willing to say no. Be willing to expand any limits you place on yourself. Be willing to say no to limits others have placed on you. Be willing to show up in each brand new day and really show up, like HERE I AM. REAL DEAL ME and its awesome! Be willing to try new things, take a step forward and learn and grow. JUST BE WILLING.

Once you are willing, a shift happens. Limits and things that you have allowed to hold you back begin to disappear. You experience the change, you feel the transformation starting, you feel the healing begin, and you feel LIFE UNFOLD. That acknowledgement and claiming of I AM WILLING is powerful and opens the floodgates. Much more is possible when you are willing.

Be willing to accept that life is not one straight line. It zigzags and curves and that is OK. Be willing to go embrace the curves because that is where the true experiences and lessons are!

Tool: I am willing to be me. I am willing to show up fully in life today. I am willing to...

7. 24 Hours

The day has 24 hours. We are only meant to carry that. No more.

We weigh ourselves down with the past, to do lists, the future, and try to cram 1000 things in one day. Then we beat ourselves up if all the 1000 things aren't accomplished. TODAY IS TODAY. Each day ends. Don't carry it into next day. Release, surrender, and start fresh with each new day. IT IS A GIFT.

Like that old story, when you get new shoes you wear the new shoes and use them. You don't wear the new shoes and mentally keep thinking about how your old worn out torn shoes sucked and fell apart, and think about those shoes over and over each day. That is like our spirit and mind. We carry all this stuff. Release it. IT SERVED ITS PURPOSE. Like your old shoes. It carried you. It fulfilled its purpose and taught you things. You remember it and are thankful but every single day and moment you don't drive yourself nuts going on and on about those old shoes. YOU HAVE NEW ONES TO ROCK. A new day to rock. You focus and appreciate today and right now.

8. Love

Transactional, conditional, and unconditional love. Transactional love is, I do something for you so that you'll do something for me. There is a benefit you are getting out of it. You do this, and then I will do that. You act this way, and then I will love you. If you don't do this or that, then the love and acceptance is not coming back in return. It is based on conditions. We all have experienced this in same way shape of form at work, with a friend, or relationship. That kind of love never satisfies and can create feelings of being unloved, holding bitterness, or always feeling like you owe something, like a scorecard. You can't blossom and be fully your authentic self in this kind of form.

Real, no holds barred, love is unconditional. You are loved regardless. You don't have to be something else or pretend or follow someone's lists of guidelines in order to receive their approval and love and feel worthy. There is an ease and flow of love always exchanging. When you can start to identify where in your life there is transactional or conditional love going on, you can make different choices. Real unconditional love is self-less, sacrificial, strong, and full regardless and not based on rules, a check list, or what someone receives in return. Love yourself unconditionally. That is authentic and in that foundation, you can soar beyond limits.

9. Being Born

You were born wild, free, gorgeous, and very spirited. You didn't want stuff, goals, success, and things.

We wanted love and our parents to give us 100% total engaged attention and presence and love. We get taught to want certain things, do and perform at certain things, and be a certain way with certain things. Please remember that you being born is the best gift. You still have all that amazing, carefree, peaceful, spirited love. Your beauty and power is inside of you to shine. Be confident in this. Remind yourself daily and be built on this truth. There isn't a one size fits all or one way of anything.

What do you want in your world right now? Is it aligned with what you have been taught or with what truly sings deep inside you? Being born is a gift and the world is your oyster the minute you breathed. Life is meant to be great, not just good.

If you are living your life and choices in a conditioned state that someone or something else taught you, question it. Does it deeply align and resonate with what you want and believe or are you on autopilot? What do you allow in your life and not allow according to your inner voice and feelings about it?

You being born is the gift. You are worthy and enough just because you were born. Period. Believe that. You don't need evidence and others approvals to make that true. It is truth.

Tool: What makes you smile and feel happy? What lights you up and makes you feel like YOU? Write down the first things that come up without judging it. Go do more of what you wrote down!

10. Truth

What is the truth that really makes you smile and lights you up?

Do what lights you up! Truly live today in a way that specifically and authentically brings joy to you and makes you feel alive with no explanation! Life is too short to live crappy! Live out loud! People, places, and things that click with you, ignite your energy, and get you encouraged and motivated! Laughter and fun are important! Life can be responsible, routine, and serious. You have to laugh. You have to have fun. You have to know your truth. Not his or her truth. Yours. That is what strengthens you, guides you, uplifts you, and keeps you powerful.

Rewrite and reframe where you're coming from. Always come from a truthful and place of power.

Women are strong, wise, and fierce! *Don't agree to something or do something that is not true for you.*

Don't allow something in your life or space, that isn't aligned with what you believe to be true for you.

Tool: Repeat this statement, "Only love is real. Love is the truth. Everything else I let go." Recognize and observe when you are feeling "off". Reframe that energy and make a new choice. Choose words that uplift you. List things that rock in your life and you are thankful for.

11. Find Your Tribe

People and environments that energy wise, vibe wise, and, spirit wise just click with you. It connects, adds value, supports, and feeds you. Your tribe gets you. They understand you just because, without explanation. They encourage, uplift, inspire, motivate, and fill you with love. It just flows and happens and isn't work or forced.

This might be friends, your community, someone you talk to on the phone, blogs that resonate and click with your heart, subject matter or books that jive with you, an instructor in a fitness class, or even your immediate family. Find them and call out loud to them in a prayer or in person. Receive them to come into your life. Your spirit soars and thrives way more with your tribe. You feel lighter and connected after being around or connecting with your tribe. Sometimes there isn't a language to explain it. They just "get" your energy, values, being, and spirit. It isn't forced, but there is a flow to it.

A genuine person or group of people will be open, honest, down to earth, and want the best for you in your highest highs and lowest lows. Finding your tribe enables you to be more fully you, shine brighter, and go farther in your goals and visions.

12. Self-love

One of the most important foundations, in which everything will branch off, is self-love.

Love yourself first. The whole world can applause you, and everyone can tell you how great you are. You can have the best hairstyle, clothes, and the nicest house, and be the coolest person in the world, but that will not make you happy. It will make you feel good for a minute, but it's not everlasting. Love has to start with you. Your spirit. Your inner voice. The stories and beliefs you tell yourself about you. What are they? Are they life-affirming, uplifting, truthful, and kind?

We are all spirits living in a body with organs!

A kidney is a kidney. If you needed one, a kidney doesn't care about your race, your religion, your bank account, or how cool you are.

At the end of the day stuff in your life can make you temporarily excited, but it doesn't bring you everlasting, unconditional, and secure love! If you are always chasing that stuff to feel important, you are never going to be happy.

Make sure today you are giving some love and attention and energy to how important and special and amazing YOU are, just because! Loving yourself from inside is the key to happiness!

We all can spend a lot of time, on a lot of things, but how much time do you spend on actually loving and affirming your spirit and heart?
That's your foundation and everything branches off of that! Choose good music, good food, good people, good environments, snuggles, laughing, and good energy that adds to your life!

Tool: Look in the mirror or say out loud in the car, "I am loved. I am worthy. I am important. I matter. I am amazing. I matter. My heart matters. I am beautiful inside and out." Do this a lot. It will go into your cells, your being, and you will feel it more and more. Practice it.

13. Be Rooted in Worthiness

Are you rooted in worthiness or are you rooted in scarcity?
In your relationships, career, and what life gives you, where are you rooted?
Do you think: Yes! I deserve abundance. I deserve respect. I deserve love and laughter and honor and sunshine. I deserve all that is good and lovely in my life! Yes! My friendships, relationships, and anything that I do and receive is my path which is grounded in worth. I am aligned with my beliefs and values.

Or, do you show up and think: Well if I am myself 100%, this person might not think I'm that fun or cool.
I'll look silly if I do this or say that at work, so I'll stay quiet.
If I try this I won't be good at it, so I shouldn't even try it,
If I revealed my beliefs or real self to everyone, I might seem weird, so I'll keep to myself. My business won't grow or I won't get promoted if I reveal my true core values.
I'll settle, because this is as good as it gets.

Show up in your life unapologetically, with YOUR values as the light that guides you.

It is exhausting to hustle for your worthiness, explain yourself, and second guess your intuition. You being you is enough and worthy!

You can read self-help books, you can go to therapy, you can take classes, and all of that is beneficial, but the real SHIFT is rocking your personal development journey and going DEEP in your spirit!
Practicing and learning and implementing tools to live your life joyfully, from your light, and your soul are the key.
People think if I follow these 3 steps and do these specific things then I will have all my answers and joy in the palm of my hand in one week. It is not an overnight thing! It is a process. It is small things all day every day adding up.

For example, if authenticity or compassion or integrity or kindness or honesty or good energy or family or truth is part of your values or beliefs, then they light you up. They are important to you, so let them guide your life. You can make your decisions, choices, and direction based on this. This can be challenging at times, but it always steers you in the direction of your best.

A favorite example is thinking of your life like a concert.

Where do you sit? Where do others sit? There's a critics box where people or your mind are always taking cheap shots.
Do you sit and react like a super fan

who sits in front row, clapping and cheering you on regardless.
What's your world like?

When your values steer you, you will limit and cut out unnecessary suffering or people/places/things that don't align with your values.
This creates space for people and things that make your spirit and light shine bright and be 100% you!

14. Allow

Allow yourself to feel what you feel and be what you are and meet your soul there. Sometimes you don't need to explain or have words to explain it and label it. Just allow it to come up. Instead of saying to yourself or to others, don't cry about that, or don't be scared, meet yourself there and allow it. Your spirit is allowed to cry and release, allowed to feel scared. The gift is how can we acknowledge this and then move through it.

When you allow yourself to be who you are, it is freeing.

We go on automatic pilot and think I have to do this and have to do that. Why not allow life to just flow and be? So much of our choices come from what we have been taught is success, is happiness, is beauty, is important, and more.

Have you allowed your soul to tell you what it needs, and what lights it up?

Allow yourself to honor what your soul is speaking to you. Moment to moment your soul will rise and your light will ignite brighter because you are allowing instead of forcing yourself to fit in a box that doesn't suit you. After you allow, then you can move through it. Don't push stuff down or suppress it, because it will just come back up later bigger and louder. Give yourself permission to feel what you feel!

15. Day by Day

Days are going to pass by regardless of what you put in them.
Every little step adds up. If you do a work out that is short and doesn't seem like a lot, it still matters!
Every little choice you make with food may not seem big deal at the time, but it adds up! Every time you don't allow crap or negative things in your life, it adds up. Each time you set a little boundary here and there in your life, it adds up! All these little choices add up day by day. It adds up to empowerment for you. It

adds up to big results in your mind, in your life, and in your journey.

The best tip is practice, practice, practice and make things a habit. Day by day. If you want to get good and familiar and consistent with anything ------you do it every single day ----- regardless.

Think of how you do your job or know how to brush your hair or if you want to start doing a handstand or if you want to learn to swim or you want to perfect a cake recipe, anything you can think of is practice, practice, practice. This leads to habit, habit, habit and it just becomes a way of life. No
secret formula! It is like the first time riding a bike. You do it over and over until repetition becomes habit and then you just do it and it is part of your life. *Stay motivated and know that everything you do matters. No matter how small. It all matters.*
Fill your days with things that are going to add up and be a benefit to your mind, heart, and life. You want to add value to your health, for your fitness, and your overall quality of life and how you feel!

16. Power word

What ONE word can be your power word for NOW? What you want more of?

A power word will be like your mantra or affirmation word each day.

It is a word that resonates with you.

There are so many to choose from like, flow, abundance, peace, creativity, rest, renewal, favor, ease, laughter, and more. First word that pops up for you, is mostly from soul. Go with it. Write it down in a big colorful pen. Hang it somewhere you will see it each day like the fridge, the mirror, or at work. It has power. It is life affirming for you. Your energy, cells, body, mind, and soul hear it. You can use your power word by saying it out loud, writing it down, making it a habit each day of making a new one or sticking with one, singing it out loud, and generating it. It is energizing, motivational, and will feel empowered.

Be loving to yourself and use your power word. It can detox any mental clutter and replace it with power, purpose, and good energy.

Tool: Pick a power word and write it down in big bold colorful letters. Post it up at work, at home, anywhere you will see it. Let it uplift and inspire you. Change it up every week or every month depending on what your needs are that day. Example power words: flow, peace, yes, growth, own my power, free, worthy, happiness, laughter, trust the process, only love is real, I will, I am, trust. It could be, f*ck yeah, if that makes you feel that power of might in your soul!

17. Ask Questions

Genuinely ask yourself weekly: What makes me happy? What lights me up and makes me smile? What do I really want the next 1, 3, 5 years to be about? What has worked and not worked for me the the last year? What serves my highest good? What do I want and what do I really need?
How do I follow these answers honestly and in a loving way to myself and to others?

Talk to yourself like a best friend! It might be new and a lot of emotions come up or maybe even feel like a lot of change or a lot of thinking. But, it is the best and most wonderful GIFT to get the ball rolling for your joy.

God works is in our weakness. You take the step and ask the questions that matter. You will discover your real deal self, and what you want and need. Sometimes you run on autopilot and think I want lots of money or I want the best job ever. But asking the above questions, maybe you really just want freedom, simplicity, or to feel passionate about what you offer the world. START ASKING YOURSELF QUESTIONS.

18. Forgive

Forgiveness releases and surrenders emotional or mental weight.

That weight of being pissed off, angry and holding on to crap people or places or things did or caused in your life or did you wrong, can keep you stuck in repetitive situations and circumstances and experiences.   That is not healthy, fun, productive, or worth your energy to rock this life you have!

It takes practice. Start somewhere. Forgive yourself today if you were hard on yourself. Forgive the person who beeped their horn in traffic and had a funky attitude. Forgive the person that doesn't have the same beliefs and values about kindness as you. Whatever it is. You might not forget it, but you forgive it so *you* can be clear and flowing. It is a major release and it's like you had this big bag of stuff you are carrying around, and the load is breaking your back and spirit. Drop the bag, so you don't have to carry it around while you are living your life. It frees you up and you have more energy and freedom to plug in and grasp life fully.

That is the first step to move on to the next phase of the day or your life. It doesn't mean anyone is right or not at fault or gets a pass. It means you are tired of carrying around the resentment, anger, hurt, or being stuck. You want to be present in your life right now. You can still honor your boundaries and what you allow in your life, while you forgive. It doesn't mean who/what you are forgiving is ok, not accountable or not responsible. It just means you want to release the heaviness in your mind and heart. Forgiveness opens the space for peace.

Tool: I forgive her/him for sucking and hurting my heart. I forgive her/him for not being who I needed them to be. I forgive her/him for not having the same beliefs as me about support/love/kindness/parenting/fill in the blank. In that forgiveness, I still honor my boundaries with them and release them to live their life, as I live mine with peace.

19. Simplify

If you are juggling a lot on your plate, simplify. Make a list. What is one thing each day you can re-prioritize? Reducing mental and emotional weight is part of the equation in ROCKING YOUR BEST LIFE. Physically. Mentally. Food wise. Soul-fully.

Do you have this insanely long to do list? Do you run all over town doing errands and carpool and feel wiped out? Are you cooking over the top meals that aren't fun to do anymore?

How about your workload? Can you simplify it to reduce feeling overwhelmed? How about your friends? Where there is drama and wasted energy, it is a waste. Start small and simplify your cooking, cleaning routine, work load, beauty routine, hobbies, and more. SIMPLIFY. It makes things easier, smoother, less chaotic, and more manageable. We are all about achievement and consuming and getting more. Contentment with breathing, smiling, eating, walking, loving, seeing, and being in the present moment is a gift.

Simplicity means being open to releasing those things that no longer serve your highest good. Bless them and release them with love knowing that they have served their purpose.

These things may be: old beliefs, habits, addictions & activities, high stress, toxic relationships that have had their time, jobs that no longer fulfill your soul, situations, even people or attitudes that no longer serve or bless you. Let it go. The less drama, the less chaotic energy, the less overwhelming stuff, then more space for more joy, more space to breathe, and enjoy the moments of life.

Tool: Write down some things that you can cut back on to simply your life. Example: You do less laundry, you don't make your bed every single day so you can enjoy a cup of tea, you save time by eating healthy sandwiches for dinner instead of cooking, you prioritize what calls need to be returned, etc.

20. Health is Wealth

Health is wealth. You are alive and can move and groove and each day you get 24 hours to live life! A brand new day. The world is your oyster. Your physical health. Your spiritual wealth. Your emotional health. Choose to focus on your true wealth. A life full of integrity, values, and a belief system is abundance and wealth.

Our "stuff" is not eternal but our Spirit is. True power and security and abundance come from spiritual connection and not through money, material goods, prestige, job titles or intellect. *You waking up is wealth. You breathing is wealth.* Shift your mindset to see the real wealth you have.

We all need to make money to survive in this world but not at the expense of our Soul and Spirit!

Self-love and worth is wealth. People search the world for STUFF to make them feel important and worth it. LOVING YOURSELF is wealth because you can't buy that or pick it up at a store for any price.

Building up your foundation of SELF LOVE AND SELF WORTH is greatest wealth. It is the foundation of EVERYTHING that branches off of that.

You will never feel full or happy even if the whole world loves you. YOU HAVE TO LOVE yourself.

Love, kindness, integrity, passion about something, family, laughter, compassion, relationships, kids, good health, and so much more is true wealth! Tool: What is your wealth?

21. Words

Words are how people express, communicate, and create. The word is a powerful tool because it can create dreams and uplift or it can tear down and be damaging. Words are energy. They are powerful. It could make or break a spirit. You have to speak and say out loud uplifting, life affirming WORDS. Powerful, life changing, abundant positive words, and them reap them in your life! Speak it in all your environments. Write it to yourself and others and post in your home!

Tool: It doesn't matter if you believe this at first. Say it. Practice it. Your cells and mind and soul will hear it and soak it in and believe it! You then will, too! SAY: My life is easy. I am wonderful and talented. I feel love and gratitude overflowing daily in my life. I am healthy energized and all is well. I am healed and whole and vibrant. I am important and seen and heard. Whatever you want to say; say it, create it in your mind to manifest into reality with divine power!

Each thought you have informs your energy, and your energy manifests into your experiences.

Your thoughts and energy create your reality. You say I ROCK or I SUCK, and then your experiences are in alignment with that!

Tool: Create a daily prayer or practice of asking your Higher Power or GOD to set you free from all the limiting beliefs that block you from believing in your greatness. Everything that shows up in your life is a lesson or a gift to teach you. You may not like the gift wrap it is packaged in, but it is still a gift! Learn and grow from it, to be a better you.

Higher Power gifts come in many forms. Maybe you have a crappy friend. It brings up for you all the other crappy friends you have had, and now this one is the icing on the cake, for you to heal, cut ties, and move on. If you lose your job, maybe you can switch career paths, learn self-empowerment, and activate your strength and resilience.

Trust the gifts that life presents to move you ahead and blossom your real deal self and greatness.

Choosing the words of how you see situations in your life can uplift you or defeat you.

22. Reframe

Reframe means change your view, change how you think or see something so you receive a better, more positive, applicable result. Change your perception. Example: You don't have a car and it sucks or you are happy to be on foot, walking to your destination, enjoying the beautiful weather, and thankful you are healthy and have both legs. If you look at things and reframe your perception, life is blessing you and teaching you.

Instead of labeling things bad or good, reframe and think this is a lesson, a teacher, and just information you are receiving along your journey. THAT IS A GIFT. Choose to see things from a positive and growth perspective.

Practice reframing things. It will elevate and uplift you. When you get in this reframe energy, you just live in it. All that is going on outside of you doesn't affect you as much, because you are coming from a reframed and uplifting perspective and energy.

Tool: Stop and recognize when you are stuck or inner critic happens. Observe and notice you are doing it.

Reframe and choose different thought or action that serves your highest good and blessing.

23. Show up as yourself

Show up as YOU in the meeting, in the store, on the bus, in your relationship, in the class, at school, and EVERYWHERE. When you are showing up as YOURSELF, awesomeness just happens! Don't pretend to be someone you aren't. Don't be fake. The storehouse of blessings will align and flow into your life, when you are being you. It will feel right, easy, and effortless.

Becoming your real deal self is a journey. You experience stuff all day that can reveal it. What you choose to think, say, feel, wear, talk, and choose INTIALLY in a split second. That is YOUR intuition. Not because someone or something or the worlds opinion told you to think this or that, but your inner compass directed you. Listening to that INNER VOICE. YOUR SOUL. YOUR SPIRIT. It reveals magic and truth and light specifically to you and in a way you hear and understand.

You might not have words to express it. It is just a soul thing. That is your authentic self.

What makes you tick, come alive, what you are passionate about, what you like and don't like, how your voice sounds, how your facial expressions come about, what music you dig, why you choose the hairstyle you dig, what your favor color is, how you hold the fork when you eat, etc. Listen and honor it. Don't shut it down.

Embrace it. Show up with that guiding you and your life will unfold with more joy, more blessings, and more I LOVE LIFE moments. It is like a radar because you are putting you out there, so what you attract back is your energy match. You like rocking bright red lipstick, or saying ya'll all the time because it comes natural? DO IT. *Being you is a gift to yourself, the world, and it allows others the gift of being themselves too.*

Tool: What screams you? What do you like to wear? Listen to? What is awesome about the sound of your voice? What is powerful about you?

22. Visualize

Visualize the smells, the sounds, the colors, the words, the people, the physical, the feelings you want to experience. Use a journal, a poster, a vision board, sticky notes, pictures, whatever you can use. If you want to travel, buy a suitcase.

If you want kids, buy diapers. If want to meet the love of your life, buy a photo album for your future pics together. If you want to own your own business, get business cards and sketch out what the space looks like.

"You have to create a vision, walk in that direction and keep dancing—no matter what." Wayne Dyer

Part of visualizing is clarity. Start making decisions, whether it is with fitness goals, life goals, and desires by your instinct and soul versus OLD HABITS AND OLD PATTERNS that NO LONGER SERVE YOU. Your life will change.

Let's say you want to get in shape. Maybe back in the day, you ate certain things because that is what your family fed you, or you only knew one way to work out or it was a season in your life back then that something worked for you. That was then. What about today? Choose different today for what works for you, today.

Today you can reprogram and choose a new habit and a new behavior. Clarity, Visualize, and Action!

Get really clear.

Example: You always celebrate a promotion, a birthday, a success with a store bought cake.

Stop and get clear. Notice that is what you do. Say, that no longer serves me today. It is not how I want to feel and this won't help me reach my goals.

Replace that old pattern with, today I will make a homemade healthy cake or instead play fun games or create a new custom for birthdays that we have never done before to celebrate.

Tool: Stop and notice and get clear on an old belief. Replace that belief with a new one that uplifts and works for you today. Practice this over and over, until it becomes a habit. DO IT EACH TIME. This increases confidence!

23. Affirmation

An affirmation is a focused declaration of energy.

There are all kinds of affirmations: "Something amazingly awesome is going to happen to me today. Life is good. I am thankful for being me. Everything comes to me easily and effortlessly. My life is blessed by divine order, divine time, and divine blessings. I am happy and thriving."
Say this daily! Out loud! Focus on the good, always. Make it a habit.

Life really is good. Go outside and stretch your arms up to the sun that comes up every day without you having to pay for it or ask it to. Pump your hands and sing song loud in the car. Today right now is a beautiful gift. You can go touch the ground outside and feel being alive!

"It's the repetition of affirmations that leads to belief. And once that belief becomes a deep conviction things begin to happen." Muhammed Ali

One of my favorite affirmations is, the Anointing of Ease. It's when you feel a Supernatural grace and feel lighter. Your load finally becomes lighter. God makes rough places smooth. No matter what Higher Power you believe. YOU ARE LOVED AND the favorite child. YOU are Apple of His eye. Everything in your life is important! Problems you may have had for a long time will be resolved and YOU will be flooded with blessings. We all have weathered rough storms and sleepless nights but your anointing of ease ALWAYS comes. God/Your Higher Power will go before you and smooth your path.

Everything will fall into place. You will receive breaks that you never imagined and blessings beyond your dreams. Believe this.

Affirm, proclaim, and declare positive things for your life.

Tool: Look up affirmations, daily devotionals, or inspirational quotes. Look online, find books, listen to podcasts, motivational speakers, go to library, write your own, find art that speaks it, and make it part of your everyday life routine. What is one thing you can do right now for this?

24. Purpose

YOU ARE POWERFUL! You are important and you have a unique purpose here on earth! YOU ARE GREATLY LOVED! Never think twice! Make sure you are around people and environments that remind you of that daily! Don't be average, be excellent! If anything in your world makes you question that then see it as a spiritual lesson to challenge you to make change. Take action to live life out loud, happy and being you!

Seriously, allow each day to feel awesome to wake up. Awesome to see what miracles and divine blessings and opportunities and people and things are going to be in your day!

Wake each day feeling gorgeous, healthy, happy, and motivated. Feel deeply profoundly important and loved. You are SEEN AND A GIFT to the Universe because you just are!

How you look, talk, walk, live, breathe, think, speak, and exist is a gift unique to you!

We all are good at things. You can be good at math or cooking or fixings things or organizing. We all have talents and strengths like being reliable or outgoing or funny. We all have personalities like being sweet or kind or energetic. YOUR PURPOSE is more meaningful and profound than all of the above.

Your purpose is unique to you and why you were born to ROCK THIS UNIVERSE. It is spiritual. It is huge. It is specific and amazing to you and out of the trillions of people in this world, no one else has your purpose. Holy moly! That is magical and special! It is higher and wider and more supernatural and important that your personality or talents or what you are good at. Being funny is awesome, but your purpose is more profound than just being funny. That might be the tool or resource you use to DELIVER and LIVE your purpose.

Discovering your purpose is key.

Most of the time it is as natural to you as breathing, but you miss it because you think it is this intricate puzzle you must figure out.

<u>Tool:</u> List everything that screams, you! Personality traits, way you talk, and walk, what you do easy as breathing, what makes you feel alive and enjoy and gets you excited and passionate.

25. Detox

Moving, grooving, and sweating. It changes you. It gives you a release and renewal. Sweating, crying, or releasing any crap inside makes you feel better mentally, emotionally, spiritually, and physically. If you can do a quick workout that will benefit you head to toe. It gets blood pumping, get cells rocking, and gets you de-stressed. Sweat it out. You feel a release, and feeling of being invigorated and healthy. This isn't about losing 10 lbs. though that will happen. Make fitness be about moving.

Fitness means moving and grooving and releasing and having fun. I always say, you have to sweat or cry to detox and release. Fitness can be fun and different each time. Walking, dancing, crawling around on the floor with kids, parking farther in the parking lot to walk more, raking leaves, going up and down the stairs for a bit, and more. It is a release. It keeps you young, refreshed, healthy, energized, and powerful and strong.

Singing songs at top of your lungs, writing in a journal words, poems, song lyrics, raps and rhymes, drawing/art, venting to someone you trust, crying with tears that flow, laughing uncontrollably deep in your belly, or dancing/running and just releasing in a safe way, detoxes you. You feel a weight has been lifted.

Tool: Go for walk. Do 10 push-ups, do stretches, put on a song and dance your pants off. Doing one thing a day, adds up to 30 days in a month of moving, releasing, and detoxing. BOOM! That is huge.

26. Food

Food is to nourish and feed you more than just because you are hungry. It isn't about counting calories or eating less. It's eating and making great choices to truly feed you nutrients and vitamins and energize you. Sometimes there is so much info out there, you think you are doing great, but you aren't because you are misinformed through advertising, books and media that are telling you crap!

Holistic real deal eating food is to be enjoyed and make you feel awesome!

Plain and simple, the sun feeds nutrients and vitamins into REAL FOOD.

You eat that. You want to feel energized, clear, and healthy. Real food rocks your bones and ligaments, your metabolism is high, you feel better, and you aren't starving, and fights diseases and sicknesses!

Eating sugar makes you feel crappy. Eating certain things, you know after you eat it, you feel funky.

Each little choice you make, can add up to great benefits. Feed and NOURISH your body, your mind, and your soul with real food, like fruit, veggies, whole grains, and food that grew out of the ground and not produced in a lab with chemicals.

If you can cut out white flour, sugar, wheat, and soy to start out, you are rocking your health. If you want cookies, make them from scratch and cut back on the sugar and use brown rice flour. Drink more water. Make vegetables exciting and use them in your pasta sauce instead of just eating them plain and steamed. Want fries, then eat real ones, not the drive thru.

Tool: Drink water right now. Today commit to drink lots of water. It is do-able. Read ingredient labels just to empower and educate yourself on what you are actually putting into your body. Decide to cook and try a new easy recipe that will feed you or your family in a healthy way.

27. Spirit

My favorite! This is way bigger than just moving, grooving, thinking, planning, and filling up with lessons and knowledge. It is about ACTIVATING your spirit. What makes you tick? By getting IN TUNE with your true nature, true joy, true UNAPLOGETIC self, what makes you glow, feel peace, feel happy, feel purposefully, and feel ALIVE, you are activating the best gift of unconditionally love to yourself.

Sometimes we all get lost in hustle and bustle of taking care of everyone, being responsible, and going with the world's flow, that our inner shine dims. We forget what makes us glow, what we are passionate about, and what makes us, US. We can be and live in world, but not of the world.

Your inner shine matters. It leads you towards the best for you. Always ACTIVATE THAT.

I am here to remind you and ignite that. Your spirit and your light will set you free and lead you best!

Certain things make you come alive with overflowing energy and passion.

When I hear certain music it fires up my being, when I dance, when I am on the beach and in the water, when I am snuggling my family, when I am trying out cool eye makeup, when I am laughing loudly and uncontrollably, when I am motivating and inspiring someone, and in my purpose and flow, when I am cooking, when I am passionately expressing my views on a specific subject, especially God and faith, when I am mommy-ing, wife-ing, sister-ing, and daughter-ing, when I am hearing or watching comedy, when I am praying and talking to God, when I am expressing myself in any, shape or form (visually, verbally, physically, emotionally), when I am lost in a good book, when I am with my family, when I am trying something challenging and adventurous, when I am smiling and loving others, and so much more. I FEEL MOST LIKE ME.

Tool: What makes you feel like you? You just know because your soul lights up and all flows and feels right with world. There are no right answers, only what is right for you. Allow yourself to talk or write this out. Give your life space and time to make connecting to your spirit a priority.

28. Micromovements

How familiar is this? I am too tired, to do that. Once the kids are older, I will take a class I wanted to do. Once I have more time, I will take a vacation. Once I have this, then I will do that. Just going for a walk today, isn't going to help me lose 20 lbs.

Brainstorming or breathing for 10 minutes one time isn't going to help my business or personal matters.

Every little micromovement adds up. Micromovement or a mini-movement or mini-step. It is small action-based choices that add up to momentum and results towards your goal.

Each day when you do one little thing, like showing up for yourself, drinking water, sticking to a boundary, taking steps instead of elevator, saying no to something without explaining, saying yes, making your own meal instead of eating out, or spending 2 minutes doing an affirmation. It all adds up. One day turns to 4 days to 4 weeks to one month. Just think if you did 30 little things through the month that seemed so small and not grand enough for impact, but it added up. It adds up to hugely and beneficially to you!

It adds up to MASSIVE stuff that will CHANGE AND ALTER your cells, your mind, your spirit, your joy, your fitness, aka YOUR LIFE!

It's amazing what happens when you are PUSHED and ELEVATED.

Your fullness and light SHINES CRAZY BRIGHT!

Micromovements are do-able. They are small. They don't need huge amounts of time and space and planning.

They are small and can be done every single day. They enable you to feel accomplished. They add up.

Tool: What are 3 micromovements/mini-movements you can do this month that are short, sweet, and easy?

29. Momentum

Even the most successful, happiest, and rocking people in the world planted seeds, then take action to gain momentum in their lives.

Planting seeds, cultivating, watering, and planting the seeds are the foundation. It is key. It creates momentum in your life and goals. *Momentum means movement, increase, and forward movement.*

It's very powerful that when you plant a seed. It could be the most bizarre out of this world thing, but you just plant that seed and you keep watering it and you keep mentioning it and you keep affirming it and you keep saying it and you keep fertilizing it. This creates momentum for outside forces, people, places, things, and Divine power to bless, bloom, and create a result. It can blow your mind. Things do happen and blossom.

Example: You want a new business location, but you can't afford it right now or can't find one that suits you. Plant seeds to anyone and everyone you know. Say I am looking for a business location. You don't need a plan. You need the intention. Every time you talk to anyone, mention this goal of yours. It might take two years. Planting the seed, watering it, and cultivating it with words, acknowledgement, affirming it, and speaking positively about it, creates momentum.

The result might not be overnight or this massive over the top result. Just daily, weekly, and monthly planting seeds. SIMPLE. Someone might say, my home has commercial approval, want to use a room? Maybe a friend says, my friend is dating a real estate agent that specializes in that. Maybe someone says, my dream is to open a business too, can we co-create? Now, even if it is not the result you want, it can be another result closer to your goal. Put that seed out there. Maybe someone else would hears your ideas and consistency, and thinks I want them on my team because they are a go getter. Your job is to plant the seeds and water them. Then, trust the blossoming process.

Finally, detach from the outcome and allow Divine Guidance to bless it.

It doesn't mean it's easy and it doesn't mean it happens in a short-term way. It could be a year it could be two years could be three years, but anything really is possible.

Momentum means movement is happening behind the scenes and it is not standing still. Yes!

This applies to meet someone amazing, a new friend, a career change, or relocation to a new town, or anything that is a desire and goal.

You can have big, juicy, huge goals and by taking the steps to plant the seeds, you are adding momentum and action and movement to them in a big way!

Tool: Keep your attitude that the world is your oyster. Plant seeds, small persistent ones and affirm them. Allow what is meant to be to be.

30. We all have a story

Your story is yours. Do you share it through writing in a journal? Share with close friends you trust? Share with people who you think it will bless?

However you choose to share your story, it is authentic to you! Are you conditioned to replay same old story in your mind, that doesn't serve your highest good?

Examples: No one cuts me a break. I have to prove myself. Money doesn't grow on trees. No one really likes me. I am not enough. Success means a cool job and lots of money.

An example: "No one cuts me a break". Maybe growing up, no family or friends encouraged you. Maybe it was a rough time at school or your home life. You felt like you had to do everything yourself, and it felt like it was you against the world. You thought, what the f*ck, someone throw me a bone!

Ask yourself, is that true today? Most likely, that story is no longer true and does not serve your higher good! Random days, you might feel that old story creep up, but it don't let it stay! Like when you first have a baby, or get a new job or you get overwhelmed and life is hard. You might think, What the heck? Anyone throw a bone? Like seriously!

Start a new story, with a new practice, which becomes a habit. Your new belief is: Life and love and God DO bless and support me fully and divinely! I get a lot of bones thrown my way!

Tool: Step 1- Stop and observe you are telling a story that does not serve your highest good and is not true for you today.

Step 2- Say: "This story does not serve my higher good and is no longer true for me." Step 3- Speak gratitude that doesn't serve that story. Step 4- Let that momentum of gratitude fuel you.

So your gratitude that serves your new story could be: listing people that have returned your calls, a friend you that really impacted your journey, someone who gave you diapers when you had your new baby, the grocery clerk that asked if you wanted help taking your groceries to the car, a co-worker that told you a compliment, a book or song that came to you in the right place and the right time, and any stand out gratitude moment small or large. This adds momentum to your new story and fuels your new belief.

This one amazing time, I was handing out food samples in NYC at a grocery store and this sweet, kind-eyed bag lady saw me every day.

On my last day working that job, she came to me and said I saved this up for you during the last month, get some food (I was eating the samples) and she gave me $3. That $3 was like $100 to her and I!

Tool: Thank you all the angels along the way who went out of their way for you and blessed you. Rewrite your story when the time is the right time for your soul to move on to the next phase of healing and serve your higher good.

31. Be Responsible for the energy you bring into any space or situation

We have no idea what someone is going through or what's on their plate or what their life is about that specific day. You can be a person of responsible energy and always come in to a space with love, kindness, and compassion. Be humbled, present, and contribute love to the person or the situation always.

Example: You go to work and a co-workers comments or energy that day wasn't cool towards you. They gave off smart comments or rolled eyes. This is perfect example, of being responsible for the energy you bring into a space.

So let's say behind the scenes at that time: You experienced loss in the family, your partner is overworking, your kids

or pets are sick, your car broke down, you didn't get much sleep, and a lot is on your plate. BE RESPONSIBLE FOR THE ENERGY YOU BRING INTO A SPACE.

You still come to work, not fake like all is perfect, but also professional and doing your job with grace and showing up. You still owned your energy you brought. So what's responsible and awesome for that co-worker? They say hi, or say good to see you today. We all choose to let our energy or words be loving. Maybe they can say, hey, I have no idea how your personal life is, but hope it is great because I know life can get overloaded for all people. Totally different attitude and energy you are bringing into the space. People can feel your energy. Right?

You be the co-worker to someone else.

We can't control others and their attitudes, but we can rock ours. I want to bring joy and love into a space. This could be at the grocery store, work, classes, school, banks, doctor offices, the park, and more. BRING LOVING ENERGY TO ALL SITUATIONS. You might be the only angel, or smile or laugh or love someone feels that day!

That is impactful! Don't assume if someone seems great and happy on surface that nothing you do matters. Don't assume if someone seems disconnected that nothing you do matters.
Be responsible for the energy that you bring into any space or situation.
What I'm really saying is don't forget who you really are. We get caught up in these roles of: look how cool I am or I have this title at work or I have it so rough or no one has it as rough as me or let me protect myself and be all bad a&& because something is making me feel insecure.

When someone gets to you just remember this: it's about them, their ideas, beliefs, values, and way of seeing the world and has NOTHING to do with you. It's their STUFF they are projecting on you. Don't let them steal your light. Move on, move through, and be a light.

I've been in mansions where the actual toilets and sinks are made of gold. I've been at the highest high with people in my career, the coolest parties, and at the most elite events with what society thinks are important people. I've also been with people struggling, and they had no shoes or coat in the winter, and crying my soul out with people who have experienced extreme life devastation and loss.

See where your energy lies. Be responsible for it.

Things and stuff don't impress me. I don't look up to people or think they're better or amazing because they are rated famous by society

or because they have a work title or because they have a brand-name purse. It doesn't matter what environment you're in or who you're around or what you have. *The true gift* is if you have love and laughter and a connection. A real authentic soul connection when you're laughing and sharing and truly living life is the richest you can ever be.

Any situation is a party, anyplace can be at home with whoever you are with, because love is there, and in any situation you get to choose and see the positive, optimism, and possibility. That's what makes people achievers and visionaries and warriors! You are responsible for your energy, heart, and what you bring. Rock that responsibility because it contributes to the greater good of the world.

Tool: Look at everyone today or the person next to you and know that everybody has stuff going on and some is overflowing and some is overwhelming. You can't control others, but you can be responsible for the energy you bring.

Be the person that brings love, kindness, humility, encouragement, and inspiration to another.

32. A-ha Moments

These are those moments when all of a sudden something RESONATES WITH YOU. Stop, notice, and celebrate it. Don't judge it or put a name to it or need evidence or a reason of why you reacted and felt something. That is your spirit. Our mind wants and needs proof. How about instead, just let it be what it is. Your personal guide and spirit.

Notice it, don't apologize or justify or explain it. Embrace it. Write it down, say it out loud, feel it and don't push it away. The more you do this, the more room you allow your inner compass to guide you. These a-ha moments are times when something just clicks and makes sense and blesses you. You feel empowered. You feel like a light bulb went off. You feel like your soul and mind connected and understood something meaningful all at the same time.

39. Your mind

You are what you think. Period! You are divine. You are amazing. You are wonderfully created! You are loved!

What's your inner voice telling your brain?!

Do you notice people can say hey you; you are gorgeous or super smart or so awesome, and if you don't think that yourself, then you don't really believe it.

What you train your brain to see and believe is what you will see and believe.

If you think positive, you will see the positive. If you think I am awesome and powerful, you will live that way. We think we have to do certain things to be loved, liked, blessed, or experience the goodness of life.

Well just because you were born and are alive, you are blessed and aligned with light and love. You have to believe and say it in your brain and walk in it. Your blessings have your name on them. Period. Seriously. They do. Remember you are a SOUL having human being experiences. On a daily basis, put good thing in your mind. Speak with power.

YOU ARE IMPORTANT AND MATTER.

Never lose that fact and place it in your mind and take time to root it there and in your heart. Your heart. Your soul. There the magic happens.

Tool: Say: All is well and flowing and peace and balanced and clear! You are what you think.

"To be yourself in a world that is constantly trying to make you something else is the greatest accomplishment." Ralph Waldo Emerson

33. Busyness

Be gentle and loving to yourself. Especially, being women and mothers and wives and girlfriends and sisters and workers and daughters and grandmas and friends. A lot is going on. Things can get too busy real quick. Stopping, noticing, and breathing to take time for you to just go slower. Cook a delicious meal not rushing through it. Stay longer in the shower, turn phone off and take a break from social media and updates on everyone's life. Don't cross off every item on your to do list. Flow with the day and allow space for random miracles to happen.

If you don't take care of your soul or body, then you can't be energized, peaceful, and in a helpful space to be your best and to rock in others' lives. Breathe in abundance. Breathe in that all is well and exhale anything that doesn't serve your highest good in that moment! Being busy is not a badge to wear and say look at me, I am so busy and I do so much, so pat me on the back.

I used to take pride back in the day, in working nonstop, and taking on an overflowing plate and saying I am superwoman look at me. It did not serve my highest good. It didn't allow me to be present in the now and soak up in of all the goodness that presented itself, because I was burnt out and tired all the time. Being busy creates the space to miss a lot of beautiful and loving moments right now in front of your face.

Tool: Start now by putting down this book, or focusing on your breath and go out and climb, touch, hug or just be near a tree and breathe in what they provide to the world. They are beautiful, they clean our air, provide a place for kids to play and animals to live, they shade us, and are rooted and strong in weather. Put your hands on a tree and be open to the stories and love and teachings it has for you.
Swim in the ocean or watch the water and how it soothes your soul. Watch a bee land on a flower or an ant crawl around in the dirt. Stop the busyness and plug into the moment at hand.

34. Empowerment

Here are some ways to be empowered. Know your identity: What you give 100%, who you are into work, family, friends, current experiences, your hobbies, etc. That is you're your real deal foundation and core of who you are.

So according to the day, the month, the peak or valley of that experience, you will feel your worth based on that. Example: what if you climbed the corporate ladder and gave your all to your current job and then the ladder fell overnight and you are unemployed. What if you repeat old tapes someone told you in past, like a teacher perhaps saying you aren't a good speaker or a parent said you aren't enough unless you have this degree. Maybe you define yourself in your talents, like I am funny, I am good at planning, I am the crafty one, or I am the dependable one.

YOUR IDENTITY IS DEEPER, much more profound than that. When you wake up daily putting your sole identity in that, you will feel empty or filled based on that day or circumstance.

Your core identity is SPIRITUAL and it is your purpose for being alive. Place your identity in something unconditional not circumstantial.

35. Inspiration

Living inspired means living IN SPIRIT. That is waking up each day, excited about your life, your world, and who you are. It has nothing to do with how much you worked out, if you slept 8 hours, or the schedule of activities for the day.

You just feel this sense of being connected and excited and inspired. It is an energy, a flow, and deep conviction that sustains you. There is no limit to inspiration. It is endless and moves you.

36. Purpose

We all have talents and skills. We have things we are awesome at and we call that our strengths. Your purpose is even greater than that. It is why you were created and brought into this world.

For example maybe you are super funny and great at storytelling. Your purpose is more than just being funny, just being smart, and just being good at something. THAT IS A SKILL. You were created for a purpose that is uniquely to you! It is what you do naturally that adds value to the world and a greater service. If you are funny and make people laugh that is awesome. The greater gift is if you use that humor to uplift people and cheer them up in a specific way that only you do.

Usually your purpose is just like breathing to you, that you miss it. Your purpose could be talking, inspiring, storytelling, loving, comforting, cooking, and being kind, giving, listening, organizing, leading, beautifying, and more. Things that come natural to you but offer a great service to the world and people's lives, or your own family, is your purpose.

When you go through trials with ups and downs, the purpose of those valleys and peaks in life is to learn and grow. Really! We all go through them. Weed out what specific seeds are yours: Seeds that were planted in your life at some point, uniquely to you, and then realize your valleys you go through are CULTIVATING TIMES for a reason to BLOOM those seeds. Boom! Powerful truth!

37. Mentors

Anything that uplifts, ignites, motivates, and adds value and wisdom to your life mentors you. Read books. Listen to podcasts. Look at art, listen to music. ANYONE or ANYTHING that FEEDS YOU. You feel better after you received the knowledge and info. It builds you up. It puts a wind in your sail. Nature can inspire you. There is good counsel from sources you respect and admire and grow from. Choose good counsel, empowerment, and love that fill you to empower you to go next step and feel beautiful inside and outside. *You are the 5 people you spend the most time with. That fills your mind, cells, and attitude.* Mentors can be books, speakers, a wise friend, a coach, a family member that inspires you, or a blog that speaks your language and opens your mind to growth. Growth is key.

You want to learn and grow from their wisdom. You feel value added to your life because of them.

38. Honor your story

Each person's struggles, falls, joys, and blessings are part of your story.

Our journey is so purposeful. Stop yourself for moment and appreciate that it's so precious. Some people have no idea they're beautiful and that their specific trials and joys bless and teach others, plus make them even more beautiful and have depth and soul. Some are busy being not beautiful because they think "if I only have this or that going for me, then I will be beautiful". If my teeth were whiter, if I lost 10 more pounds, once I get my degree, if I fix my hair better, if I speak more eloquent, if I try harder, and fill in the blank.

You are beautiful because of your stories, experiences, character, integrity, beliefs, and scars. They make you real, authentic, relatable, and phenomenal. Don't get caught up on the surface or comparison or the worlds standards, because you lose your unique beauty and soul.

We all have a story of where we come from, what we went through, what we experienced that was rough and tough and beautiful and blessed.

It is yours to honor. *Never forget where you come from and what made you become who you are today.*

Your story is a gift because it most likely has some profound storms and triumphs. Honor that. It might have sucked, it might have been unplanned, it might have been upsetting, it might have been amazing, and it might be all of those. Honor it. It served its purpose in your growth, it gave you character and soul, and it can or can't define you. It is always your choice. Never be ashamed of your story or fear the truth. Your story is your story and can be honored. It can be used as fuel to further you in your journey and dreams for life.

39. Roles

Mother. Wife. Best Friend. Manager. Daughter. The funny one. The organizer. The short one. The go getter. The hard worker. The cute one. Office Assistant. Getting caught up in a role, can hold you back from the real deal you and limit you.

Think of experiences that give you a feeling of contentment, like being in nature, or listening to the birds, or the sound of the waves, or contemplating the stars in the night sky, or watching your child sleep, or being with your dog or cat, or maybe it's when you look in the eyes of a loved one!

Those experiences that touch your soul! They light you up in your heart.

Ego is who you think you are. How do you identify yourself and thoughts about different roles that you play in society? Every one of our roles is a thought or a form. Sometimes, we confuse ourselves with the roles. Some examples are: I am from California. I am a mother. I am the manager. I am a vegan. We are much more than that.

Instead, live from your soul and open your heart. Soul to soul. When you go the bank, or grocery store and exchange hellos and communication, just think everybody is a soul. You are exchanging energy. Our mind labels and thinks they are customers and they are workers. Why not think, we are all souls living in this world, doing our best to give love, be love, receive love, and live life happily and best we can. Let's contribute and help each other in that.

If you have kids, your kids are souls. They are sweet, pure, untainted, heavenly souls to LEARN FROM. They are in the role of children and you're in the mother or father role, but we are all souls exchanging wisdom, love, and purpose.

40. Divinity

Your foundation daily is YOU ARE DIVINE. You were made in the image of GOD/ a divine Higher Power that created you with brains, beauty, talent, gifts, love, wisdom, and kindness. Especially when things are rough or tough, come back who you are. YOUR DIVINITY.

Repeat to yourself: I am special, awesome, divinely created, and NO ONE CAN TAKE THAT AWAY EVER. Maybe circumstances or situations or people challenge or affect our brain away from that core, but come back to your truth.

We are amazing spirits HERE TO ROCK THE WORLD AND SERVE a specific fabulous specific purpose.

Tool: Remind yourself you are made from the Divine and you are amazing. Don't define your worth and divinity from your circumstances. Your foundation is holy.

41. Habits and conditioning

Read this over and over the rest of your life! *It is golden.*

Every single person, all people have their own set of belief systems, rules and procedures that define if a person is loving or good or bad, or how life should operate.

If you do or don't follow it, your value goes up and down based on the system others are operating from. Are you allowing that to control your value as a person?!

There is a story of a pro athlete MLB player who pretty much said: He was a professional baseball player and every time he won a game, he felt great and was happy and his teammates wanted to party with him and celebrate him and companies wanted to do business with him, and he made money and felt important. Then every time he lost a game, everybody was disappointed in him and his teammates were pissed and didn't want to hang out, and he felt like a failure. His family thought he might lose his job and the coach was disappointed in him and his value was that he was unimportant and sucked.

He said, he lived his life up-and-down every day in his 20s allowing his value as a human being to go up and down based on that system and it was an upsetting, anxious, and conditional way to live! *Your gift today, is to know your value internally.*

For you to know you are important and be at peace with exactly who you are is a gift, because we live in a society where we are so conditioned by our family, the world, society, and what we were taught at home, religion, school, and the news--- we continually get challenged on that system.

Your value doesn't go up or down based your how many Facebook likes you have, how many books you sell, if you get a raise at work, if you lost or won game, if you won an award or if you are single or get married, or if your parent thinks you are a good or bad person.

Do you have a peace about things in your life? Your marriage, family, kids, career, friendships, how you talk/dress/eat, your purpose, your character, values, my decisions, what you bring to the table, fill in blank, who you are.

Your value is unchanging. It is unconditional. Allow nothing to alter your value and importance. Feed, nourish, and cultivate your value, your heart, and your INNER SOUL. Everything branches off of that.

Your value is divine and powerful because you were born and unconditionally loved. You are a spirit and a soul and a beautiful gift to world. Being born is powerful. That never changes!

Here is the challenge, because we have to live in the world that is full of all kinds of challenges, hills, valleys, peaks, and other people with other beliefs and rules, everything constantly gets challenged. We react, we question, we respond, we protect ourselves, we freeze, we defend, we rethink things, we forget OUR VALUE and UNWAVERING truth. Remind yourself daily. Practice and make it a habit.

The good thing is that for all the crappy and rough storms and challenges, YOU are like a tree and your roots continue to grow and grow deeper.

Everything gets resilient and stronger. That means the storms come and sway your branches and rustle the limbs and move and shake but the root and trunk never break. The roots grow deeper and longer. The true withstands and grows more beautiful and produces more fruit. WHOOP! YES! You rise.

We can learn that when people make you feel bad or pound on you and hurt your feelings and want YOU to use THEIR belief system, that's when chaos happens. Remember, it's not about YOU, it's them. Stay out of the chaos.

Golden takeaway: The challenge of this lifetime is to know that we live in the world, so even though you can be strong and peaceful and hard-core on exactly what makes you happy, you will constantly be challenged by people, friends, family, coworkers, and people on the street or anywhere in life. It will hurt or challenge your ways and your feelings because we are not robots, but it will not sway your roots, truth, and core.

42. Beliefs

Beliefs can be rewired. Old conditions you were taught might not be true or serve you and your life today. Here are examples: Men leave. Money is scarce. Life is hard. Only certain kinds of people succeed. Diets are only way to lose weight. Most girls are mean.

Guess what? Old beliefs that no longer serve who you are today can be changed! How? Change your inner dialogue. Create new thinking, habits, and beliefs. You can choose to believe different and practice that new belief daily.

It's all conditioning from the way you were brought up, what society, TV, and pop culture tells you.

It's what you learned from school, sports, relationships, jobs, parents, and more. Life in general conditions you and you have to be clear and listen to your inner compass. *Ask yourself, IS THIS BELIEF TRUE TO ME? Do I value and belief that because I passionately do or because someone told/taught me I had to?*

Tool: Ask yourself in situations, "Whose driving the bus here?" Is it your ego, your 7 year old self, your teenage self, your inner wise self, your upbringing, society, or your soul wisdom?

43. Soul Signature

Your soul and your being have specific vibes and signatures. It is totally, YOU. Everything you do or say bears your signature and your being. You got to run your life by your spiritual rules and integrity! You got to run you're day to day and career/business by your soul signature. What brings you energy, aliveness, and joy? Do more of it! For example, if you don't like certain social media, stop using it. If you don't dig cooking huge meals for the holidays, don't do it and do something else.

Do more of what makes you happy because people will feed off that. You will feed off of it, and that gains momentum. People can feel if you are excited or genuine. It's contagious. Period. You can feel when you are doing something that is resonating with you or when you are being "on" and doing something to please others. When it is real deal and authentic, it's easy, it flows, its natural joy and not manufactured.

Your words, thoughts, how you treat others, how you show up, what you stand for and speak up about bears your print. Think of it like when you sign your name. It is totally unique to you.

Tool: What's your signature to this world?

44. Stand for something

A favorite quote when I was a teen I had painted on my wall in my bedroom (I had tons of quotes painted on my bedroom wall because my awesome mom who rocked empowerment) was:

"Stand for something or you will fall for anything."

Be bold and passionate about something. Don't let the world or people sway and tempt you and your beliefs. They will challenge them. Stand strong and be passionate. Usually, hardships, rock bottom, hard times, rough patches in your journey create a passion inside you.

You want to speak up, stand out on certain causes, subjects, or beliefs because you went through them yourself, and they affected you deeply. They become what you are passionate about.

Not everyone has to agree on things. That is beauty of life. You can have different perspectives and feelings about things. Passion about something is exciting because it fuels you. It ignites you. It adds value to the world, others' lives, and your life. Your passion develops because it is usually personal to you and your experience. Rock that.

45. Gems

Certain things are sacred and pure. Don't let people, society, and world convince or steal that from you. Whatever it may be. Your values, innocence, a special experience, pure thoughts, an untainted experience. Let it stay special. We are taught to get more, go faster, better, stronger, harder, and reveal everything to everyone especially social media. Keep some things as gems to yourself. We have to have some white pretty angelic, puffy cloud things that are untarnished. Hold them like jewels.

We are becoming too desensitized to life. It's nothing to people anymore to hear, see, and experience crazy crap anymore! It is like nothing is surprising. You have the power to hold on to some pure jewels! Pick and choose what you fill your mind and time with. You can decide what you watch, listen to, read, surround yourself with, and what special moments are yours to keep special. This relates to your mind, body, and soul.

46. Self-worth

Say and believe: I'm awesome regardless! I am enough. I do enough. I have enough.

We have to stop beating ourselves up. That is unnecessary suffering. Self-inflicted. What do you beat yourself over on? Examples are: not working enough, not getting that thank you card out, not eating healthier, why did I eat that extra cookies, I didn't get my to do list done, I wasn't a good enough friend, I could have done better, I shouldn't feel this way, etc.

Your worth is not based on that. You are worthy, period. You are enough. Your job is not to become perfect and flawless. You are allowed to just be and feel. God isn't up there bartering your worth! You are greatly loved period! You have breath and you exist. You are amazing. Period. Don't barter your worth. I am awesome, if I do this or that. I am important, only if this happens.

I matter, if I do that. I am strong, if I do this. No bartering. You are phenomenal. That is a complete sentence.

Your worth is to be spiritually connected to anything you do in this lifetime. Because if you're not you will never achieve your greatest gifts and blessings to give the world and to yourself. Maybe you have done the corporate thing, or the cool stuff that seemed hip in the moment, or tried to fit in when it didn't feel totally right. It served its purpose to get you exactly where you are today, to teach you profound lessons and see what works and doesn't work for you.

Once your spirit was not attached to it, and it is not right for your soul, then you make a new choice. Don't allow it to sway your worth. You are worthy!

47. Flow and Roadblocks

We all hit roadblocks. You stumble. You fall. It's hard, especially if you're doing what is unconventional or what everyone else is doing. This relates to starting a business, moving along your career path, defining your relationships, your parenting, and how you live any area of your life.

I remember at 23 years old, saying I'm going off the map, the "plan", and everyone around me, was like what are you doing!?

My career path and how I was creating my life (location, living, friend circle, career path, and spiritual path) was not what everyone around me was doing at that time.

It was hard, challenging, and I was off the beaten path. The safe path. It was not easy, but it was the best thing I ever did!

But that's what a leader is. That's what an entrepreneurial spirit is. That is what an intuitive being is. That's what a trailblazer is. That is what a truth seeker is. That is what a fire starter is. That is what a spirit shaker is. You hit a roadblock and you figure out a new street around it.

Everybody has different gifts that come easily to them. Things that flow for you are things that come easily and effortlessly. Your job is to bless and serve the world with them. Some people have a lot of family members that can hook them up, some people are financially blessed, some people talk easily, some people teach easily, some people give smiles that just light up the world, some people are great storytellers, some people are amazing cooks, some people are just awesome at being moms, and some people are really good at math, some people are great at organizing, some are great at fashion, some are great at listening to others, and on and on. There are endless amounts of things people are great at.

Whatever you're really good at, tap into it, and see it as a gift. Then share it because that's when the magic happens. Share your fashion sense so others can apply it and feel hip and gorgeous.

My mom's wisdom about life was sometimes things are going to take you longer, but you're still going to do exactly what you're meant to do and will have everything that is meant for you. It might take you longer to achieve, and might have to work harder, but the best is yet to come and you will have it all. *Your blessings have your name on them!*

A great metaphor of attitude which shows flow is imagining you are in a river, hanging onto to raft, but you know how to swim. Why are you holding on the raft then?

In your soul and instinct, you know when something or someone has served their purpose. Your spirit says I am done, so move on to the next phase or season of your journey. If you continue to be irritated, upset, frustrated, confused, and pissed off for next few months or years, it is like hanging on to a raft that served its purpose and you can swim.

You are capable and need to move on down the river to enjoy the flow of the water and scenery. Let go. You will better yourself, honor your soul, and be empowered to enjoy life and flow through your journey.

48. Abundance

Have an abundance mindset that there is enough to go around and you'll never miss your boat. Blessings have your name on it you can't miss them! There are two choices you can have. They are an abundance mindset or scarcity mindset.

Life is a beautiful place where there is love, possibility, miracles, joy, and fun! We must choose to see it amidst the other crappy stuff going on, too. In life, all kinds of stuff happen, but it is the meaning you attach to it.

Life is a journey with all kinds of experiences to learn lessons. What you do with the lessons is the gift to yourself. Every lesson is just information. That's all. It is information to push you into your best self and push you along into what makes your soul specifically sing. There isn't one size fits all.

God is a creative artist! Embrace that. Shift and reframe your perspective on things. You learn what you do and don't want through the lessons life presents.

For example, let's say you lost your job. Choose an abundance mindset that you are moving to the next beautiful phase of your life. Maybe you are pushed to go for your dreams or spend more time with your family, or take time to cultivate that you are strong and driven and this lesson deepens that.

Another example could be that you get lost driving and now you are late for a meeting. You still have to deal with the consequences, but your mind and attitude can reframe. Abundance mindset. You are divinely being guided, are safe and protected in your path to the meeting and now you had a creative idea because you were inspired by something you saw.

Tool: Discover an abundance mindset. What is challenging you to have this mindset? Get to the root of your idea of abundance and scarcity.

49. Energy

Have you ever been ready for a change? You just FEEL IT AND KNOW IT.

A career, a location, a situation, or a person has served its purpose. You feel disconnected and not spiritually IN it anymore. You learned and grew and ready for next step.

It is time to start listening to what your next phase of life is.
Our soul LOUDLY tells us, do this, do that, this no longer serves you, you can't grow here, do these 2 hobbies you've loved since childhood, slow down, don't date this person, you really want this, and more. Our brain wants evidence. Our brain says things all day to quiet that shouting! We make reasons and

excuses of why we can't or won't.
We ignore it. Our soul, our inner wise
self, and our instinct are so crystal clear!

Our inner compass is an abundance space. All things are possible and it delivers wisdom, passion, and direction easily. Sometimes people don't want to shine light on those parts because it is work to make it happen into life. That might entail more communication and change and new environments and new everything. IT IS WORTH IT.

Vulnerability is part of the equation, and sometimes is a little harder because you're not going the way the world is set up but you're going the way God set it up. Soul says stuff easily and effortlessly, but then you have to make it function in this life we live called EARTH!

It is a beautiful thing to have courage to do what makes your inner drum beat and roar. Do it! What contributes to the world in a beautiful wonderful way is when you are being YOURSELF, you you you.

The way you talk the way you dress the way you speak the way you present yourself the way you deliver the way you receive the way you give in the way you do things has that stamp of you on it!

It's awesome when you have 100 certifications/degrees, and you've paid for marketing classes and art classes and all of these things to perfect you and better you. These are beneficial, but also remember that you are just to take gems and nuggets out of those experiences and put them in your tool belt of your tools that you used to live life.

When you deliver something in your way people resonate with that and so do you and its more authentic it's more successful and it's more contributing. It has energy. Don't ever become a way that you think you're supposed to be at work in a relationship in your life socially or anything because you're missing out on your flow of energy into world.

50. Inner compass. Spirit. Soul. Instinct. Higher Power,

Your mind doesn't always understand your inner compass. Your Soul may tell you where to go and what to do without explaining why.

Following it, will lead you to peace, release, and you. Practice it in the small things and it becomes a habit.

When you live your life based on rules, beliefs, and habits that society /family /someone else pounds into you, and it doesn't resonate and work for you, then you will suffer. Do you make choices and live your life by your own beliefs and listening to YOUR integrity? *Listen to the beat of your drum or you will be living in unnecessary suffering and/or chaos from trying to live someone else's way, while your soul is shouting for its voice.*

Tool: Breath. Listen to beat of your heart. Don't think or plan or question. Feel your heart beating. Just be.

51. Support and rest

Support and rest can profoundly change your life. Support looks different for everyone depending on what your life is like.

For example, maybe you are a mom who busts their booty all day at work and comes home and is depleted. You still have to cook and clean and be a mom with kids running around and your brain is mush. You need support.

Maybe your career is your passion, and you work all the time and give until you are empty. You need support. Maybe you are lonely and bored and want more friends and want more excitement in your life. You need support.

Maybe you live life a certain way and feel disconnected from other people because they don't see things like you do. You need support. Your mind races and runs when you're trying to go to sleep at night and you wake up feeling like you never went to bed. You need support. You take care of the whole world but don't ever put your own needs first. You need support.

Support means finding your tribe. Your peeps. Your people. Your vibe of like-minded and like souled people, places, or things that feed you, add to you, and carry you in ways that support and add to you.

Rest will regenerate your cells, your soul, and being. It will do things for your heart, your brain chemistry, your body, and your well-being in magical ways that nothing else will. When you rest you're allowing everything to take a break and let your body's natural functioning work at its best. Rest can mean, shutting off your phone, staring at a tree and plugging into nature, focusing on your breath and listening to it, reading a book you enjoy, staying in the shower longer, lying in bed even if you don't sleep, and anything that allows your body and mind to be quiet, stop, and just be.

52. Self-support

Today do some form of self-care or self-rest or self-love or self-support. Be aware and notice that you are doing it for yourself. Hurray! Be excited that you're doing it and depositing love into yourself. See how you feel before and after you do it. It could be reading a book or blasting music in your car and singing at the top of your lungs, just because you want to and it feels super! It could be saying no to a party you don't want to attend or letting the dishes sit and housework not be done because you want to take a nap and just rest in bed. Do it!

If you're mind starts that inner chatter where old tapes start playing of the self-critic, which tries to sabotage it and say, you don't have time for this, who are you do to this, etc. then:

Go back to the reminder of your inner compass.

Your mind won't understand your inner compass. Your Soul may tell you where to go and what to do without explaining why. Follow your inner compass! It always leads you in the best and highest good for you.

This could mean take a bath instead of a shower. Stay in the shower and don't rush out and just breathe. Turn your phone off, make a meal from scratch that nourishes you, recite affirmations and talk to yourself in the mirror and say I am beautiful and awesome, sleep and take a nap even if it is 15 minutes, say no with no explanation, let your to-do list wait for another day, sit in your car after work for 10 min and just breathe or listen to music you like and don't rush into the house.

Self-support doesn't always mean just taking a bath or sleeping in an extra 10 minutes because it is a good thing to do for you. It can mean grand things, like not allowing someone to bring chaos into your life. It could mean saying no to extra hours at work and choosing your family over the extra money because you know it will be too much for you and your health will be affected. It could mean not allowing a friend to always complain and drain your energy every single day, and choosing to cut back and choose to be filled up and uplifted instead of drained. Small micro movements of self-rest will alter your energy and day for the good.

53. Life lessons

In different phases of your life you are learning loads of wisdom and life lessons about relationships, people, work, yourself, and your journey.

You might not even realize at the time you are learning golden gems. Sometimes we are so focused on this "set" life plan that things will be a certain way, that we miss out on the blessings and then golden gems that are happening to us. We don't really "get it" or soak it up and feel the empowerment and majesty of it all.

In any situation, always ask yourself, "What is this here to teach me?" If that seems incomprehensible at the time, still ask yourself the question because it is shifting and opening the space for the gems to appear to you.

We are rigid sometimes, like this is the only way that career, love, friend, and life wise stuff is going to happen. If there are stumbling blocks or things not falling into place along the way, you think-- something must be wrong!?

Nope, you are in the box that was created. It's ok.

That's how journey goes. That's how we learn and grow and expand.

Try stepping outside the box and try a different way of seeing things. You can be IN the world, but not OF the world. You start to feel more like yourself. You see what works for you and doesn't.

You see what expands and you see what constricts.

You see what inspires and feed you, you see what drains and deducts from you. It is life. You gain and lose friends. You get wild, and you get serene. You have highs and lows. You experience blessing, and you experience heartache. Things fail or people fail you. It's ALL part of it. Everyone experiences it. What can you learn from it?

I am built for this kind of stuff.

It is what you do with it. Don't toss it to the wind. Use it, apply it, and be wiser because of it. Does it increase your depth? Does it make you turn to your spirit? Does it ignite your purpose YOU offer life? Does it increase your gratitude? Does it make you really LIVE out loud and vibrantly? Does it make you love even more? Write down and honor YOUR LIFE lessons you have learned to be TRUE and WISE through your life and remember them and live them. Keep a warrior attitude that you are built for this kind of stuff and will grow and rise because of it.

54. Love & honor yourself (before you can love and honor another)

When you embrace all of you first, then you can truly love and get excited about your career path or a relationship or life in general. It just flows. It's anointed. It's affirmed. It just IS.

Because life is going to continue to keep going and there's going to be ups and there's going to be downs. There's going to be beautiful things and shitty things. The rest of your life! But if you get into your SOUL and love and honor it and yourself, you will see it all as an experience. It won't throw you for a massive tornado loop. You will still feel and express and sometimes it will suck, but you will learn from it and let it add depth and character. The life tools will be added to your toolbox for going through life.

You will still feel it but in a more divine way. You will feel spiritual lessons. It goes beyond the surface. You will be with it, as opposed to it's out there, and you are in here. You are with it. The laughter, and the crying. The understanding, and the frustration. It deepens your spiritual practice. Deepens your love, your gratitude, and something magical happens, and you feel it.

You can actually feel angels and divine presence and an energetic heavenly power throughout the process. This is empowerment for you.

You choose to be of service to the world and to inspire the world through your OWN eyes and experiences you have.

Embrace you, step aside the box, and inspire the world being apologetically YOU!

55. Encouragement

Who do you surround yourself with, what feeds you through the day? An environment and energy that is supportive, uplifting, encouraging, good energy and nurturing will take you WAY farther than vibes that are constricting, manipulating, negative, and nagging.

ENERGY THAT IS SUPPORTIVE AND UPLIFTING WILL TAKE YOU FAR.

Each thought you have informs your energy, and your energy manifests into your experiences. Your thoughts and energy create your reality. You say I ROCK or I SUCK, and your experiences are in alignment with that!

Sign up for free newsletters from a motivational person, read uplifting books, surround yourself and your environment with colors and pictures that make you smile, listen to music that uplifts you, get outside in nature in any form you can, or get magazines that interest you and push you to be your best and support your dreams and goals.

When you're encouraged, you vibrate energy of confidence, love, support, and motivation. You just know it. Any disbelief or lack or questioning wilts away, and is replaced by encouragement and inspiration. When you feel that deeply inside, you live it.

56. Change your perception

There are choices all day to perceive things with a positive attitude. For an example you don't have a car. Your choice is that is ok for right now because today you are happy to be on foot, enjoying the beautiful weather, not spending money on gas, and getting your blood pumping while everyone else is stuck in traffic and you are walking/biking. Another choice is complaining about how unfair your situation is. Choose that you don't have a car now, but you will. You are thankful to be walking/biking, and you are planting seeds towards your goal of having a car.

Choose the positive, and remember there are other people that are hustling hard in the direction of the better life they desire.

Wishing with all of your might and complaining will do nothing to improve your life if you're not willing to back up your words with big time action. Choose a positive perception and take little action steps daily towards your goal.

Ask yourself what is really important and have the wisdom and courage to build your life around that. *You can't control anything except the meaning that you give things.* For example, you get laid off from your job and you can't control that. You can control what the meaning of that means to you. It could mean you can now get a new job with better hours in the direction of your career goals. It could mean you are learning resilience and tenacity. It could mean you get extra time in the meantime to spend time with your family.

The way you communicate with yourself and talk to yourself is important. Instead of a why me thought, think what can I learn from this. Instead of thinking this is horrible; choose to think, this can be a blessing for my greater good. *Ask a lousy question get a lousy answer. Ask an empowering question and add empowerment to yourself.*

How come I can never lose weight your brain will tell you because you suck. If you say instead how can I enjoy the process of working out and eating better? Your mind will give you positive feedback like maybe you cannot diet but replace certain things

It's in struggle that we grow. It's a challenge, and challenges are exciting. Don't let rough patches squash your enthusiasm.

Rise to challenges. Don't get pushed back by anything. Miracles are natural happenings operative through spiritual forces. If you only understand life through your senses, you'll think it's something contrary and won't see the miracles. When trouble comes think of all you have to be thankful for and praise, praise, praise! All day every day, your attitude allows you to soar or defeat in any situation! Reframe your thinking when needed!
Be bold. Be beautiful! Be thankful! See the blessing! Be motivated to live TODAY laughing, happy, moving,

grooving, healthy, passionate, and alive. Breathe. Repeat.

Tool: The way to remove mountains is the way of praise! Say thank you, speak gratitude, and learn from the struggles and grow stronger and motivated.

57. Values

You can desire stuff intellectually and want stuff like a house, a new friendship, or a promotion.

But if your belief system, your actual belief doesn't believe you can have that, then you won't have it. Your inner being has to believe it, and be it. The great news is beliefs can be rewired. Old conditions you were taught can be changed!

Old beliefs that no longer serve who you are today can be changed! Change your inner dialogue. Create new thinking habits and beliefs that are true for you.

One example is how you value your worthiness. So for example, your value doesn't go up or down based your how many Facebook likes you have, or how many books you sell, or if you wear a certain size, or if you lost or won a game, or if you won an award or if you finally get married or if your parent thinks you are a good or bad person. Fill in the blank.

It's all conditioning from the way you were brought up society, the media, sports you played, or just life in general. Choose your new belief about value and practice it. What is your new belief about being worthy? You are a tree, your roots are STRONG. Your branches may sway, and even break off and get rustled, but the sun still shines and you are strong. You will still bloom, grow, expand, and stand tall. Spiritual warrior. Life warrior. Love warrior. A warrior. You are worthy because you were born and that is enough. Practice your new belief about your value.

58. Boundaries

If someone, something, a circumstance, an action, or anything makes you feel "off", or is not adding good energy, positivity, or connecting to you, or is constricting you or creating drama or chaos, you can allow yourself to create boundaries. They reflect your worth and how you value yourself and your time and what you will allow in your world.

You deserve to be living life as you, and being happy, feeling uplifted and loved and not drained or beat down, or defeated because of someone else's "stuff" or energy- sucking vampire ways. The more you surround yourself with people, places, events, and things that are more LIKE YOUR REAL DEAL SELF, the more life is fulfilling, exciting, and flowing.

Don't let anyone or anything BLOCK YOUR FLOW, your blessings, and your REAL DEAL loving, powerful self.

Think of boundaries like a fence you put around your house. The fence is there to keep your home safe, peaceful, clear, and uncluttered. It is your responsibility to enforce the fence.

If someone throws litter in your yard, you have to re-enforce that you don't allow litter in your yard, and the fence represents your space.

Boundaries can be simple or grand, depending on where on your journey you are placing them.

The more you practice boundaries, the more you feel empowered and create what your soul and life needs.

59. Self-care

Being women, mothers, wives, girlfriends, workers, daughters, grandmas, sisters, and friends mean a lot is always going on. Remember to Love yourself. Allow yourself to take time to cook a delicious meal not rushing, or stay longer in shower or turn the phone off and just be
or if you have an extra 10 minutes, sit on the couch and don't feel like you have to call someone back or use your time doing something constructive. Don't make a to-do list one day and just flow

and allow life to unfold without an agenda. Surprising miracles happen.

True self care is listening to and nurturing your own needs. Being hard wired to be a "good girl" or the "nice one," doesn't mean putting your self-care last on the list. Practice radical self-care for yourself today!

60. Breathe

Think about trees. They are beautiful to look at. They clean our air, and provide a place for kids to play, and providing the building materials for our homes. Trees give off oxygen just before dawn, which wakes up the birds and makes them sing! Cool, right?

Put your hands on or hug a tree and send your gratitude back to it! We hardly think about this stuff.

When is the last time you stared at how majestic trees are, or how the ocean soothes your soul or actually watched a bee land on a flower, and then plugged into that moment? That is practicing mindfulness. Be really in that moment, aware of all the feelings, smells, and sounds of it. Life is busy and rushed. The easiest place to start is breathing.

Seriously, this might be challenging. To sit still, lay still, BE STILL and breathe. Breathe in your nose and out of your mouth. Breathing is happening tens of thousands of times every day of your life. Events of your life come and go, and nothing stays constant because everything is changing through the day, but your breath is consistent.

Life can get hectic and become just go-go-go. Even if your life is awesome and fabulous, it can still be busy and full and fast. Stopping to notice and plug into your breath, you enter in that space of calm, no worry, no anxiety, no comparing, and, no doing. It's healing to your body, your cells, your heart, and your BEING.

Use a word that works for you. **Breathing, meditation, prayer, sun salutations, getting quiet, resting, quiet time, going inward, centering, God, Higher Power, angels, calm energy.**

Tool: Make this a daily practice to quiet down and connect to your breath, nature, a tree, a bee, something that allows you to be and breathe and be in the moment only. It can save your life, better your life, center you, and bless you. Try 10 minutes of "centering and quieting" today.

61. Spiritual laws

There are spiritual laws always going on regardless if you believe they work or if they work. When you understand, believe, and plug into them and have faith that they work on your behalf, life changes. You are not separate from God, or others, or people. We are all connected. Everything has divine time and divine order. The sun rises, the moon sets, there are 24 hours in a day, and more. What you put into life, you get back from life.

SPIRITUAL LAWS ARE IN OPERATION.

Become aware of them and allow them to flow and work on your behalf simply because you are aware and honor them. Notice how the sun comes up and moon comes out.

Notice that there are only 24 hours in day, so why try to work and carry the load of more than that.

62. What you eat

When you eat fresh real whole food, you feel energized, vibrant, and healthy. It sounds so easy and basic. When you eat a huge Thanksgiving dinner with potatoes and stuffing and turkey, you're ready for the couch afterwards. Then you say," I ate and feel exhausted! I can't move! I am never doing that again!" That's because you're eating white flour and white sugar. Your cells and your body and your muscles and your stomach are speaking to you and feeling the results of that! White flour and sugar will kill your energy, metabolism, and immunity strength.

When you choose to cut back on sugar and white flour and processed foods and fill your body with whole, healthy, vitamin-filled foods that nurture your spirit, mind, and body, you feel energized! You feel healthier, trim and fit, and strong!

Sugar is in everything. It is hidden! It can cause pain and disease. It can contribute to inflammation, major weight gain, immunity strength, and your affecting your energy levels.

Yes, vegetables and fruits are wonderful, but think outside of the box. You can enjoy all kinds of foods like bread, pasta, and desserts. Don't you want to eat cookies and enjoy bread? By just choosing and replacing the ingredients, changes everything.

If you eat a ton of cookies and a big huge sub you will feel one way! Bloated, yucky, and crappy! If you make homemade cookies with coconut oil and flaxseed meal, and dairy free chocolate, or make a loaded sub with fresh pesto, fresh tomatoes, and a good bread choice you feel totally different! Energized, clear, filled, and satisfied!

Food is to be enjoyed and received with love as it nurtures and feeds your brain, body, and spirit.

Making replacements and little choices add up. It can change your brain, metabolism, and turn you into a fat burning machine full of energy and clarity, and pain and disease free! Who doesn't want that?

Tool: Start by reading ingredient labels on your food. Learn what hidden words mean sugar. It is hidden in everything. Find a recipe that is easy to try for your favorite dessert or meal with better ingredients. (For cutting sugar, and more nutrition in detail or recipe books www.theswstudio.com)

63. Move and groove

Moving is considered going for a walk, dancing in your house, taking the stairs, parking your car farther to get to the store, taking a fitness class, cutting the grass (with a push mower, people!), running around after kids, biking outside, hiking, or doing a DVD.

When you move, you are feeding oxygen and energy to all of body and organs. Your brain wakes up, you're getting your blood pumping, and you're getting your ligaments and muscles lubricated. You feel awake and it's making you feel alive and everything is functioning better.

When you sweat and when you're breathing heavier than usual from a work out you are doing so much!

It is a stress release, plus it's important for your mind, body, and soul. You are stretching your joints, you're burning body fat, you are keeping your organs rocking at their best, and more importantly you're keeping yourself young and vibrant and healthy. You always feel accomplished when you move!

A healthy self-esteem is the best gift to yourself!

Start moving and grooving in any way that brings you joy. Walk with a friend, or maybe go outside and run after your kids or listen to music and start dropping it like it's hot. If cleaning your house is fun to you, then make it a workout! Don't plan on doing it, don't start tomorrow. Take action now! (Go ahead. Do some jumping jacks)

64. Expression

Expression: Whether it's talking, writing, moving, art, the way you dress, the way you cook, the way you do anything- that is an expression of you is very important to living an amazing life.

Everybody has an authentic unique: Vibe, walk, talk, look, voice, perspective, thoughts, ideas, OVERALL VIBE AND SPIRIT! What screams you?

Are you a homebody or have a cool haircut going on or do you have a soft laid-back vibe or do you love to design and paint or do love to cook or are you super talkative and passionate or you have heart for those in pain, or are you reserved and a loner, love rock music or country, have a poetic side or want to be a lounge singer?!

Whatever is unique and authentic and makes you feel alive, expressive, and real deal you; do more of it every day!

You are special, you are magnificent, you are a warrior, and there's absolutely no one else in the world like you!

The world needs more of you! *The more you fall in love and become more of your true real deal self, then the more easily your life will flow.* BLESSINGS AND MIRACLES AND GOOD FAVOR with your name on it will flow easier into your world. All aspects of your life will start to fall into place because you're just putting out energy that's natural. It is just you being you. You won't have to question things because you're being you and you're attracting that in your life.

65. Gratitude attitude

Just being thankful all day and every day no matter what occurs in your life can change the entire dynamic of your life.

A thankful attitude changes relationships, it changes your mood, it changes your attitude, it changes the way you see the world. Get out of bed and say, thank you that I got to sleep last night, and that I had blankets, and that my feet, hands, organs, head, and eyes are working to get out of bed.

Thank you for food to eat. Thank you that I have shoes to put on my feet and I can walk and move. Thank you, I woke up today and the world is my oyster!

Say thank you at the store, thank you to your family, thank you to your kids, thank you to the person that drives you crazy because you can always learn a lesson from them, thank you that the sun rises and the sun sets and you did nothing to make that happen, it does it regardless. Thank you that spring is after winter. Right? That is awesome!

Gratitude will change your life.

Proclaim to the world that something unexpected, exciting, and amazingly awesome is going to happen to you today! Your mind is a powerful tool. Purposely put loving, grateful, thankful, positive things in there! Write it down. Say it out loud! That puts it into the world and in a form and generates more of it. The fact you are alive, reading this, and can breathe and move is something to say THANK YOU for. Tell someone, I AM THANKFUL I AM ALIVE and WOKE UP TODAY. More you say it, more you will feel thankful for it.

Tool: Instead of looking for problems, look for new blessings! Every day tell yourself three pieces of amazing awesomeness! Pick 3 blessings that are different than the day before. Blessings move mountains.

Praise moves mountains. When things seem rough, PRAISE and start saying out loud what is FREAKING thankful and incredible in your life. It reframes your energy, your focus, and your attitude!

Stop and really truly connect to your breath and say thank you that my organs are working and that I'm breathing. Being thankful can change everything. Life becomes a beautiful experience no matter what! You become a warrior and life is a treat!

66. One new habit

Just to show how powerful and magnificent you are, pick one little habit to do every day. It could be saying thank you every morning when you wake up. It could be writing a little love note to family member and leaving it for them every day.

It could be packing your lunch every day instead of eating out. It could be spending 5 minutes each morning in silence thinking of your blessings.

One little thing that you can do every day. This will show you how powerful you are! Your life is a canvas waiting for you to paint it with beautiful colors of your words, your actions, your choices, and what you put to action!

It can be a huge masterpiece art piece that's blowing your socks off or it can stay blank! It is your choice.

You have the energy, the light, and the talent to do it no matter how busy or where you're at in your life! One new habit to create and bring into your life forever to bring more love, more sunshine, and more good energy in your life. You can do it!

67. In tune

Get in touch with your deeper self. Prayer is speaking and talking and communicating through words, arts, music, thoughts writing, feelings, movement. or through any kind of expression that feels right for you! Connecting or talking to your Higher Power, God, Jesus, Universe, Inner

Wise Self, Instinct, Inner Compass, Spirit, Soul, Inner Knowing, or something bigger than you that is your SOURCE!

When you feel stuck in your journey or you're having a frustrating day or you feel lonely or feel pissed off or misunderstood or you feel like you don't know what the next step is in a relationship or in your life or just in your spiritual journey, TUNE IN.

Prayer changes everything because it's like an electrical plug, and it plugs you into your Source that created you. That is your Divinity. It doesn't matter how old you are or who you are or where you are you in your journey. You are important, powerful, and loved. Imagine not even tapping into that. You have something bigger and better and greater operating your life!

Tap into that greatness. Be still and think about it. If this is foreign to you, go in nature. Put your feet in the grass or watch the sun rise or the moon and stars. There is a huge universe hat is beautiful and YOU ARE CONNECTED TO THAT CREATION!

68. Morning

Your morning is setting the tone for your day. Get into a schedule or routine, so you don't feel rushed. You want time to have a great start to the day that is full of positive energy and a great attitude.

Be sure to have a routine which still leaves time for you to say an affirmation, stretch, have a tea/coffee, or whatever you need to do that SETS the tone of sunshine for your day.

It's important to say an affirmation or say a prayer or take five minutes to start your day saying something like, "I'm thankful. Today's a brand-new day of possibility. Everything comes easily and effortlessly to me."

Today is full of blessings and miracles and laughter. This day will be filled with good people, good things, and I embrace and receive it. I'm excited and thankful to live this day boldly and with expectancy of great things." "I am a warrior. I'm a rock star. I am unapologetic of the love and goodness that I'm bringing to the world today!"

Hug and kiss and say I love you to your pets, your family, your plants, your roommate, whatever home is for you, and to yourself. *Be love, spread love, give love, talk about love, put that energy all around you first thing in morning because it will generate and radiate tenfold!*

The morning sets the tone for the rest of your day, so choose to start it off with gratitude, time to give love and receive love and fill your cup with a positive attitude to rock the rest of the day.

69. Write it and say it

Remember in school, teachers would say "Here are 10 definitions, please write the word and write the definition." And you think, okay that's homework? I don't have to memorize anything or study, but just write stuff?

Or way back in the day, they made you write on the chalkboard 50 times, I will not chew gum in class.

The purpose to this is when you write things and when you speak things out loud, it changes the actual cells and energy of your entire being. You feel it, you become it, and it's a lot easier to actually BELIEVE IT. DO IT. FOLLOW IT!

If you make it a practice of writing or speaking out loud, I am blessed. I am thankful. I am vibrant. I am healthy. I am alive. I am making great choices. God has my back. I am happy. An energy and a momentum attaches to this. It has a vibration and a power that brings it to light and is way more powerful because it is in a form which is written or verbal. It is not just in your mind as a thought.

Anything you want, Write it and say it!

You will actually see your attitude and your day change and be blessed and full of miracles! You will feel different! You will feel the release or the power of it once you put it into a form.

One of my beliefs is that no matter what's going on in your life, even when you're not feeling great or things are sucking, you still need to say and speak victory. *Words are powerful.* They change your being, and they affect your deep inner soul and they can either vibrate and uplift you or bring you down.

Your subconscious mind soaks it, regardless of if you think it is doing anything. ROCK THIS!

You can have all the love and admiration from the world and people, but if you don't love yourself, none of it will make you happy.

70. Let your talents be of service to the world

We all have talents and gifts. Change your outlook and your perspective of what these talents and gifts are for. Instead of what does the world do for me? What can I get out of this person? What is my work doing this for me?

Frame the question to yourself and shift to a place of service. You are blessing the world with your gifts, talents, and heart. Your voice, your heart, and your being are blessing this relationship.

It is rocking your work environment. It is spreading your energy in situations. Appreciate that you are bringing specific talents and personality and gifts to work today. You matter and count. You are contributing to the world by being you.

Your smile can rock someone's day and make them feel sunshine. You being good at anything and everything, adds value to other people. It adds value to the world being a better place. It adds goodness to situations. It is bigger than just blessing your own world. It is blessing everything around you.

This attitude opens up opportunities. It opens your journey to receive more blessing, joy, miracles and a deep meaningful profound gift inside your spirit; that money, power, fame, and titles, and stuff can never fill.

Tool: How do you show up in the world? What makes you unique? What rocks about you? How do you add value?

71. Practice, practice, practice

There is no blue print or 5 step plan on achieving the perfect job, making the best decision, finding the right person, or fixing anything in your life that needs support.

If anyone tells you follow these 5 steps and life will all be fixed and great, it is not true! *Life is practicing.* Finding tools that support, motivate, and encourage you. Practice them day in and day out. When you learn a lesson, keep practicing it. Let the lesson turn into a blessing! Like riding a bike, or learning to walk, you do it over and over and over again until it is easier to do and becomes part of you, like breathing.

Practice anything you want to get better at, improve, or master.

Life is about learning and experiencing. When you learn and gain a tool that helps, supports, or uplifts you to better yourself, you add it to your toolbox and use it again and again. Practice is taking action. We get a chance every moment to practice, make a different choice, and learn and grow in love and light.

72. Action

Taking action in your life and creating the life you want, starts with you. It starts with your inner self and attitude.

Action is consciously initiating movement.

This could be mentally or physically or emotionally. It goes beyond thinking about it, or planning it, but *actual movement.*

You get to choose to be creative and resourceful or complain about your resources.

The power is in your attitude. The power is your actions. The power is your spirit, where it is unlimited and free. You can stay in the boat or walk on the water!

Taking action in any small way to love yourself more, to choose an attitude that will empower you, and to begin applying tools for your life that will inspire and create blessings in your world, is what ROCKING YOUR LIFE means.

For more encouragement, inspiration and motivation come join our tribe:
www.theswstudio.com
www.twitter.com/theswstudio

Made in the USA
Las Vegas, NV
10 March 2023

68798723R00066